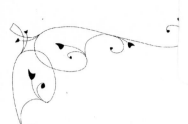

Creating An Afternoon to Remember

A Collection of Afternoon Tea Recipes

From

An Afternoon to Remember Tea
Parlor and Gifts

by

Amy Lawrence

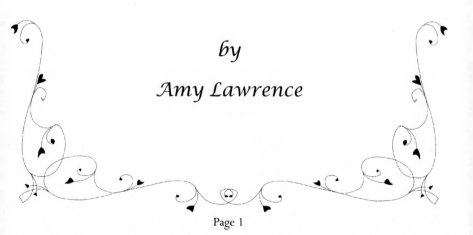

Published by:
ATR Publishing

Cover Photo by:
Raggedy Annie Photography
Annie Jornlin
(916)780-6159
Raggedyanniephotography.com

Back Cover Photo by:
Sirlin Photographers
(916)444-8464
http://www.sirlin.com/

ISBN: 978-0-9796170-0-3

An Afternoon to Remember is dedicated to educating others in the art of taking tea. Our mission is to provide a unique upscale experience where customers are pampered and can relax, socialize and celebrate special occasions while enjoying excellent teas and delectable treats. Tea rooms entice you to sit leisurely, and this is the main goal and purpose of our tea room making your experience here truly...

"An Afternoon to Remember."

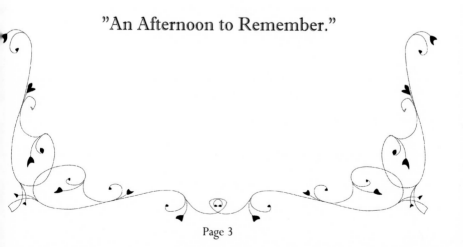

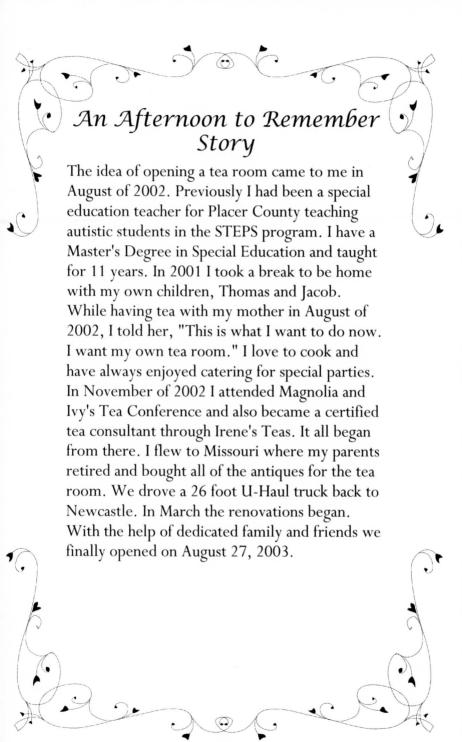

An Afternoon to Remember Story

The idea of opening a tea room came to me in August of 2002. Previously I had been a special education teacher for Placer County teaching autistic students in the STEPS program. I have a Master's Degree in Special Education and taught for 11 years. In 2001 I took a break to be home with my own children, Thomas and Jacob. While having tea with my mother in August of 2002, I told her, "This is what I want to do now. I want my own tea room." I love to cook and have always enjoyed catering for special parties. In November of 2002 I attended Magnolia and Ivy's Tea Conference and also became a certified tea consultant through Irene's Teas. It all began from there. I flew to Missouri where my parents retired and bought all of the antiques for the tea room. We drove a 26 foot U-Haul truck back to Newcastle. In March the renovations began. With the help of dedicated family and friends we finally opened on August 27, 2003.

Dedication

I would like to dedicate this cookbook to my grandmother, Alice McCoy who passed away on April 12, 2004. She is the one who inspired my love of cooking. I remember sitting on a stool in her tiny kitchen watching her make everything from German Chocolate Cake, English Dips to my favorite dish – homemade noodles.

I would also like to dedicate this cookbook especially to my family, friends and staff. Without them this tea room would not be the success that it is today. I would like to thank them all for their time, effort, support and most of all, friendship.

Table of Contents

Tea

Scones and Condiments

Table of Contents Continued

Quiche

Soups

Salads

Tea Sandwiches

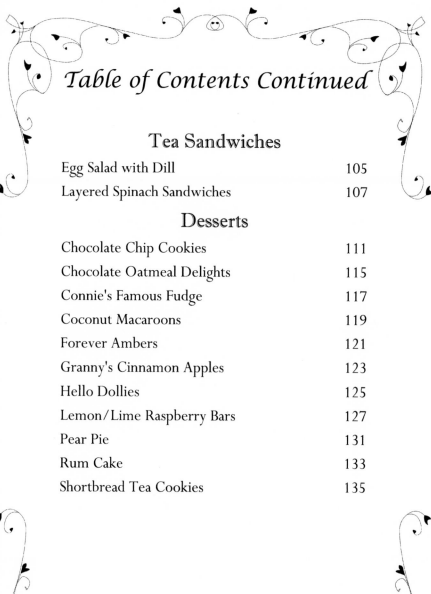

Table of Contents Continued

Tea Sandwiches

Desserts

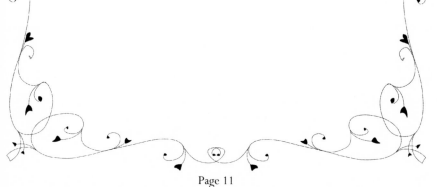

Tea

The Perfect Pot of Tea

Fill kettle with freshly drawn cold water.

Temper teapot by filling with hot water.

Bring kettle to boil.

Pour out water in teapot.

Place tea sock in teapot.

Add one scant teaspoon of tea per cup.

Pour boiling water over leaves.

Replace teapot lid.

Steep for 3-5 minutes for black tea.

Decant or remove tea sock with leaves.

Stir and serve.

Cover with a tea cozy or use a warmer to keep tea piping hot.

Enjoy!

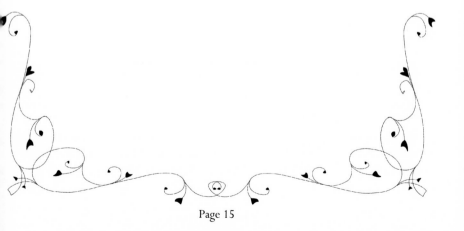

How to Decaffeinate Tea

Fill kettle with freshly drawn cold water.

Temper tea pot by filling with hot water.

Bring kettle to boil.

Pour out water in tea pot.

Place tea sock in tea pot.

Add one scant teaspoon of tea per cup. (For large pot use 4 teaspoons.)

Pour enough boiling water to just cover leaves. Wait 20-30 seconds and discard the water from the tea pot. Pour more boiling water through the tea sock and fill the pot.

Replace tea pot lid.

Steep for 3-5 minutes for black tea.

Decant or remove tea sock with leaves. Stir and serve.

Enjoy!

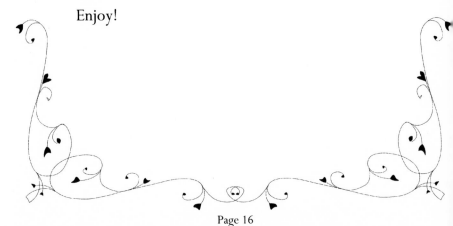

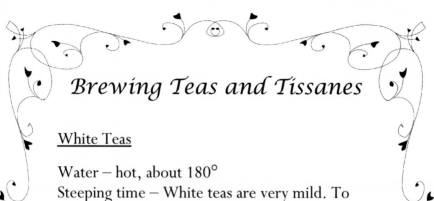

Brewing Teas and Tissanes

White Teas

Water – hot, about 180°
Steeping time – White teas are very mild. To get the full flavor, steep for 10-12 minutes.

Green Teas

Water – hot, about 180°
Steeping time – Most green teas can be steeped more than once. If multiple infusions are desired then start with a steeping time of 2 minutes and then increase it by 1 minute for every additional infusion.

Oolongs

Water – a little less than boiling – around 195°
Steeping time – same as green teas

Black Tea

Water – almost boiling
Steeping time – normally 3-4 minutes. Some Darjeelings are best at 3 minutes.

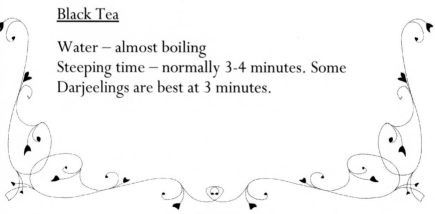

Brewing Teas and Tissanes Continued

Flavored Black Teas

Water – almost boiling
Steeping time – 3-4 minutes

Tisanes or Herbal Blends

Water – boiling

Steeping time – 7 minutes

Gourmet Iced Tea

This will make approximately 2 quarts of gourmet iced tea with loose tea leaves. Use fresh, cold water from the tap or spring water. Do not reuse water you have already boiled since the oxygen will have evaporated and this affects the taste of the tea.

Measure ¼ cup of tea leaves (to make 2 quarts or 8 cups) into your infuser. For this quantity of leaves, you will need a large infuser for the leaves to have room to expand and brew properly. A cotton tea sock or the large basket infuser will work perfectly. Use a tea pot to house the infuser and brew the tea.

Heat 4 cups of water until it reaches the correct temperature: generally, steaming for green and almost a full boil for black teas, oolongs, herbal infusions and fruit blends. Pour it over the leaves immediately and cover your teapot.

Brew the tea for 5 minutes for black teas, 2-3 minutes for green and 10 minutes for Rooibos or herbal teas. Over brewing can cause the tea to taste bitter so use the appropriate time according to the specific tea.

Gourmet Iced Tea Continued

After brewing, remove the leaves immediately.

Fill a 2 quart pitcher with ice. Pour the tea over the ice and into the pitcher and sweeten if desired. Then, add enough cold tap water to fill the pitcher. This will make a strong tea, you can dilute with more water according to your taste.

A 4 oz. tin makes about 14 quarts. A 2 oz. tin makes about 6 quarts. A 1 oz tin makes about 3 quarts.

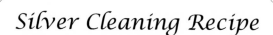

Silver Cleaning Recipe

Connie brought in this recipe and it is a quick way to clean small silver pieces – especially silverware and tiny teapot spoons.

- One large sheet of foil
- 1 c. baking soda
- Boiling water
- Tarnished silver pieces

Cover the bottom of a large plastic container with a large sheet of foil. Lay small pieces of silver on foil. Sprinkle ½-1 c. baking soda over silver. Pour enough boiling water over pieces to cover. Rinse and dry.

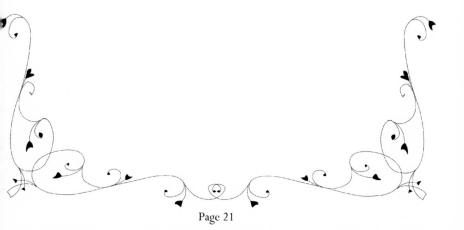

Notes

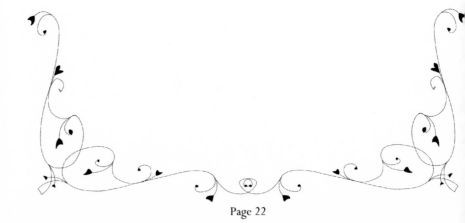

Scones and
Condiments

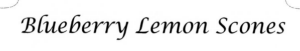

Blueberry Lemon Scones

Scones

- 3 c. self-rising flour
- ½ c. sugar
- 1 stick unsalted butter
- 1 c. buttermilk
- ½ c. blueberries
- 1 t. lemon extract
- 2 T. peel or zest of one lemon

Glaze

- 1 c. powdered sugar
- 2-3 T. water or milk

Combine flour and sugar. Cut in butter until mixture is coarse and crumbly. Add blueberries. Mix buttermilk, lemon peel/zest and lemon extract. Add just enough of buttermilk mixture to make a soft dough. Turn out on a floured board and cut with a biscuit or cookie cutter.

Place scones close together on a cookie sheet sprayed with vegetable oil. Bake at 400° until lightly browned about 10 minutes. Brush with glaze while still hot. Enjoy!

Scones are served best warm and may be reheated in foil before serving.

Notes

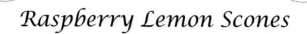

Raspberry Lemon Scones

Scones

- 3 c. self-rising flour
- ½ c. sugar
- 1 stick unsalted butter
- 1 c. buttermilk
- ½ c. raspberries
- 1 t. lemon extract
- 2 T. peel or zest of one lemon

Glaze

- 1 c. powdered sugar
- 2-3 T. water or milk

Combine flour and sugar. Cut in butter until mixture is coarse and crumbly. Add raspberries. Mix buttermilk, lemon peel/zest and lemon extract. Add just enough of buttermilk mixture to make a soft dough. Turn out on a floured board and cut with a biscuit or cookie cutter. These tend to get quite sticky so add more flour as necessary.

Place scones close together on a cookie sheet sprayed with vegetable oil. Bake at 400° until

Notes

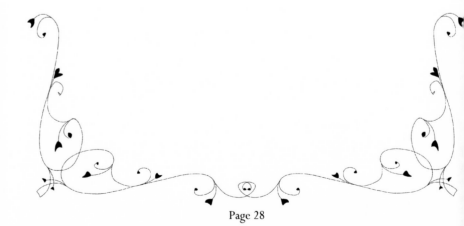

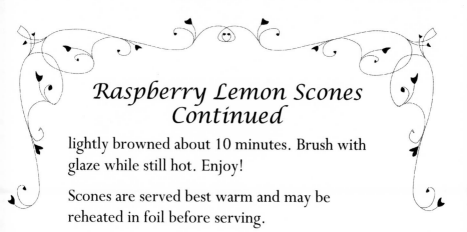

Raspberry Lemon Scones
Continued

lightly browned about 10 minutes. Brush with glaze while still hot. Enjoy!

Scones are served best warm and may be reheated in foil before serving.

Notes

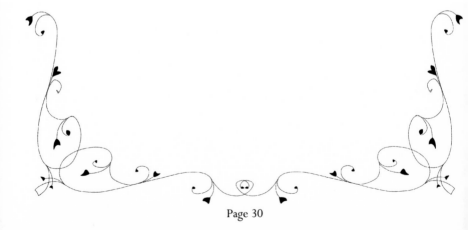

Cinnamon Pecan Scones

Scones

- 3 c. self-rising flour
- ½ c. sugar
- 1 stick unsalted butter
- 1 c. buttermilk
- ½ c. of toasted chopped pecans
- 1 T. cinnamon

Combine flour, sugar and cinnamon. Cut in butter until mixture is coarse and crumbly. Mix in pecans. Add just enough of buttermilk mixture to make a soft dough. Turn out on a floured board and cut with a biscuit or cookie cutter.

Place scones close together on a cookie sheet sprayed with vegetable oil. Bake at 400° until lightly browned about 7-10 minutes. Enjoy!

Scones are served best warm and may be reheated in foil before serving.

Notes

Cranberry Orange Scones

Scones

- 3 c. self-rising flour
- ½ c. sugar
- 1 stick unsalted butter
- 1 c. buttermilk
- ½ c. chopped cranberries
- peel or zest of one orange

Glaze

- 1 c. powdered sugar
- 2-3 T. orange juice

Combine flour and sugar. Cut in butter until mixture is coarse and crumbly. Add cranberries and orange peel/zest. Add just enough of buttermilk mixture to make a soft dough. Turn out on a floured board and cut with a biscuit or cookie cutter.

Place scones close together on a cookie sheet sprayed with vegetable oil. Bake at 400° until lightly browned about 10 minutes. Brush with glaze while still hot. Enjoy!

Scones are served best warm and may be reheated in foil before serving.

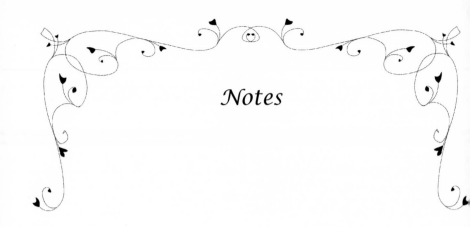

Notes

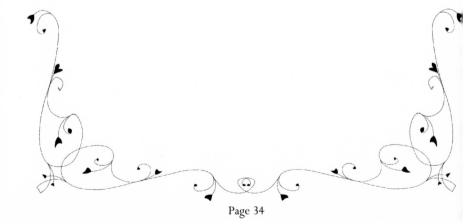

Lavender Scones

Scones

- 3 c. self-rising flour
- ¾ c. sugar
- 1 T. fresh lavender leaves or ground
- 1 stick unsalted butter
- 1 c. buttermilk

Glaze

- 1 c. powdered sugar
- 2-3 T. water or milk
- 1 t. vanilla extract

Combine flour, sugar and lavender. Cut in butter until mixture is coarse and crumbly. Add just enough of buttermilk mixture to make a soft dough. Turn out on a floured board and cut with a biscuit or cookie cutter.

Place scones close together on a cookie sheet sprayed with vegetable oil. Bake at 400° until lightly browned about 10 minutes. Brush with glaze while still hot.

Scones are served best warm and may be

Notes

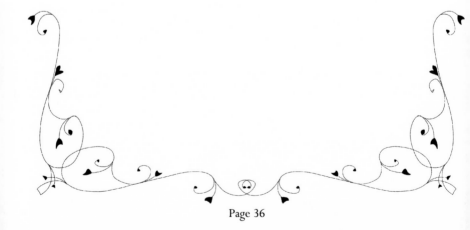

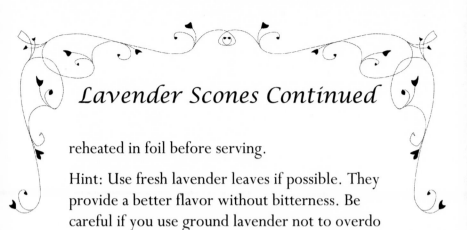

Lavender Scones Continued

reheated in foil before serving.

Hint: Use fresh lavender leaves if possible. They provide a better flavor without bitterness. Be careful if you use ground lavender not to overdo it. Too much lavender makes the scones bitter and leaves a perfume taste in the mouth.

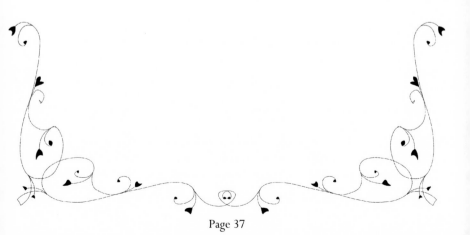

Notes

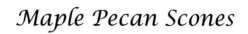

Maple Pecan Scones

Scones

- 3 c. self-rising flour
- ½ c. sugar
- 1 stick unsalted butter
- ½ c. buttermilk
- ¼ c. pure maple syrup
- ¼ c. whipping cream
- ½ c. of toasted chopped pecans
- 1 T. cinnamon

Glaze

- 1 c. powdered sugar
- 2-3 T. maple syrup

Combine flour and sugar. Cut in butter until mixture is coarse and crumbly. Mix in cinnamon and pecans. Add maple syrup and whipping cream. Add just enough of buttermilk mixture to make a soft dough. Turn out on a floured board and cut with a biscuit or cookie cutter.

Place scones close together on a cookie sheet sprayed with vegetable oil. Bake at 400° until lightly browned about 10 minutes. Brush with

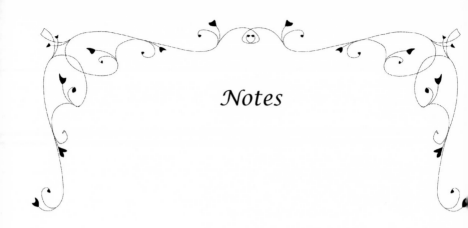

Notes

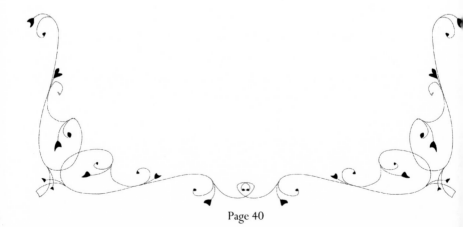

Maple Pecan Scones
Continued

glaze while still hot.

Scones are served best warm and may be reheated in foil before serving.

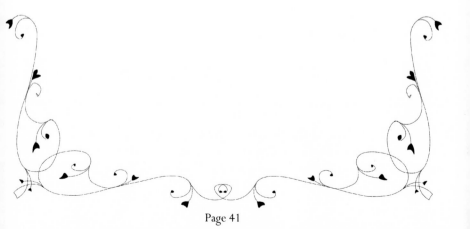

Notes

Pumpkin Pecan Scones

Scones

- 3 c. self-rising flour
- ½ c. sugar
- 2 T. cinnamon
- ¾ c. of toasted pecan pieces
- 1 stick unsalted butter
- 1 c. canned pumpkin
- ¾ c. buttermilk

Glaze

- 1 c. powdered sugar
- 2-3 T. water or milk

Combine flour, sugar and cinnamon. Cut in butter until mixture is coarse and crumbly. Mix in pecans and pumpkin. Add just enough of buttermilk mixture to make a soft dough. Turn out on a floured board and cut with a biscuit or cookie cutter.

Place scones close together on a cookie sheet sprayed with vegetable oil. Bake at 400° until lightly browned about 8-10 minutes. Brush with glaze while still hot. Enjoy!

Scones are served best warm and may be reheated in foil before serving.

Notes

Savory Scones

- 3 c. self-rising flour
- ⅛ c. sugar
- 1 c. sun dried tomatoes
- 1 t. pepper
- ½ c. parmesan or sharp cheddar cheese, grated
- 1 clove of garlic, minced
- 1 stick unsalted butter
- 1 c. buttermilk

Rehydrate sun dried tomatoes by adding boiling water to them. Allow them to sit for at least 5 minutes. Drain tomatoes and squeeze all of the excess water out with paper towels.

Combine flour, sugar and pepper. Cut in butter until mixture is coarse and crumbly. Mix in tomatoes, garlic and cheese. Add just enough of buttermilk mixture to make a soft dough. Turn out on a floured board and cut with a biscuit or cookie cutter. Spread extra cheese over top if desired.

Place scones close together on a cookie sheet sprayed with vegetable oil. Bake at 400° until lightly browned about 7-10 minutes.

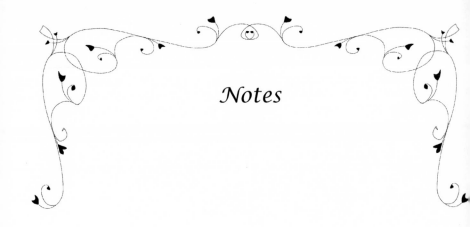

Notes

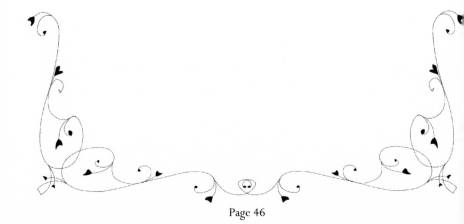

Savory Scones Continued

These are delicious with basil butter. Enjoy!

Scones are served best warm and may be reheated in foil before serving.

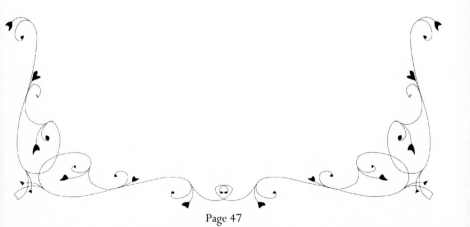

Notes

Snowflake Scones

This recipe was inspired by two of my customers.

- 3 c. self-rising flour
- ½ c. sugar
- ½ c. white chocolate chips
- 1 stick unsalted butter
- 1 c. buttermilk
- ½ c. coconut

Combine flour and sugar. Cut in butter until mixture is coarse and crumbly. Mix in coconut and chips. Add just enough of buttermilk mixture to make a soft dough. Turn out on a floured board and cut with a biscuit or cookie cutter.

Place scones close together on a cookie sheet sprayed with vegetable oil. Bake at 400° until lightly browned about 7-10 minutes. You need to carefully watch these as the coconut browns very quickly. Enjoy!

To make White Chocolate Raspberry Scones – add ¼ c. fresh raspberries and decrease the

Notes

Snowflake Scones Continued

buttermilk to ¾ c.

Scones are served best warm and may be
reheated in foil before serving.

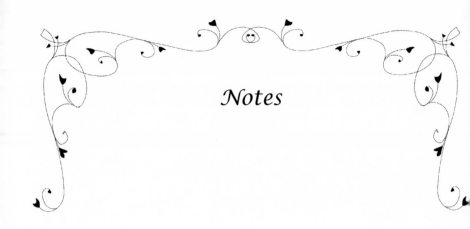

Notes

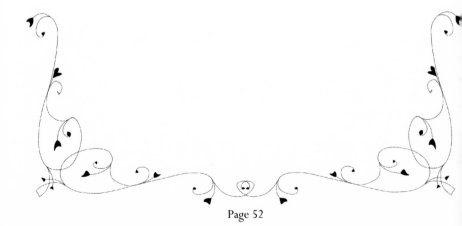

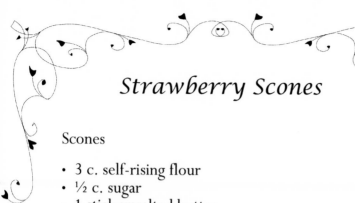

Strawberry Scones

Scones

- 3 c. self-rising flour
- ½ c. sugar
- 1 stick unsalted butter
- 1 c. buttermilk
- ½ c. sliced strawberries

Glaze

- 1 c. powdered sugar
- 2-3 T. water or milk

Combine flour and sugar. Cut in butter until mixture is coarse and crumbly. Add strawberries. Add just enough of buttermilk to make a soft dough. Turn out on a floured board and cut with a biscuit or cookie cutter.

Place scones close together on a cookie sheet sprayed with vegetable oil. Bake at 400° until lightly browned about 10 minutes. Brush with glaze while still hot. Enjoy!

Scones are served best warm and may be reheated in foil before serving.

Notes

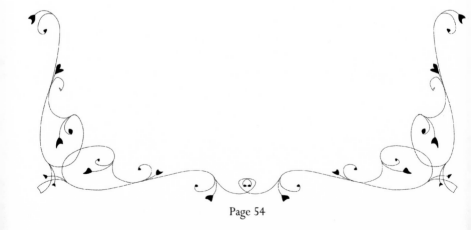

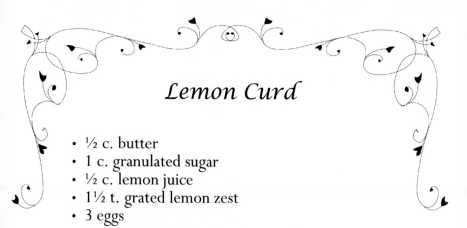

Lemon Curd

- ½ c. butter
- 1 c. granulated sugar
- ½ c. lemon juice
- 1½ t. grated lemon zest
- 3 eggs

Melt butter in microwave for 1 minute. Beat eggs in a glass bowl with an electric mixer until frothy. Mix in butter, sugar, lemon juice and zest. Microwave on HIGH for 3 minutes.

Beat mixture again until smooth. Microwave on HIGH for another 3 minutes. Beat mixture again until smooth. Refrigerate until set/cool. Lemon curd will keep up to 2 weeks in refrigerator.

Makes about 1 cup of lemon curd.

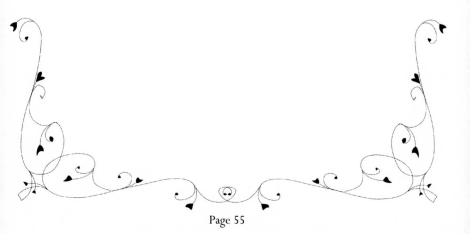

Notes

Devonshire Cream

This is not a "true" Devonshire cream, but our
customers love our version.

- 1 8 oz. pkg. softened cream cheese
- 2 c. powdered sugar
- ½ freshly squeezed lemon
- 2 t. vanilla
- 1 c. sour cream

In a small bowl with an electric mixer, beat
cream cheese, lemon juice, and vanilla.
Gradually beat in powdered sugar. Fold in sour
cream.

Makes 1½ cups.

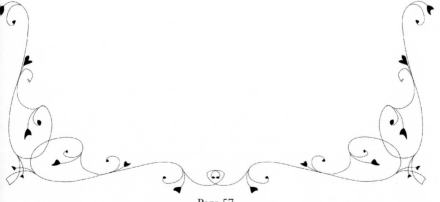

Notes

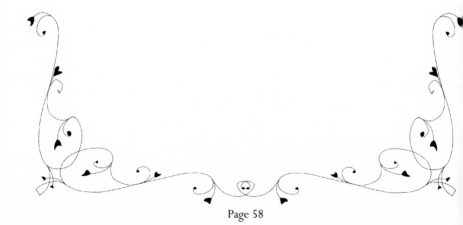

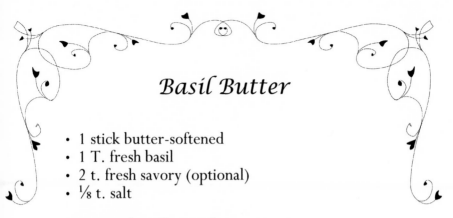

Basil Butter

- 1 stick butter-softened
- 1 T. fresh basil
- 2 t. fresh savory (optional)
- ⅛ t. salt

Mix together all ingredients. Store in refrigerator.

Mixture is best when made ahead a few days.

Serve at room temperature with warm Savory Scones.

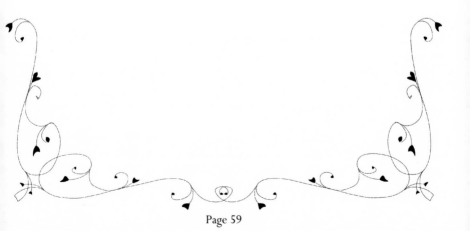

Notes

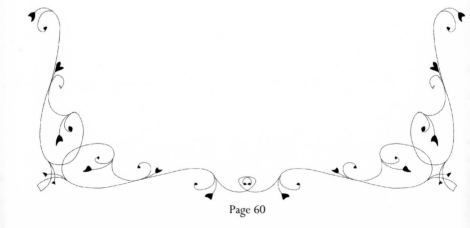

Quiche

Our Famous Quiche Recipe

This recipe was inspired by my dear friend Nancy Ellis. She made this on our opening weekend. Little did we know then that this dish would become our signature recipe.

- 2 c. of shredded black forest ham – from the Newcastle Cheese shop
- 2 c. Jarlsberg cheese – from the Newcastle Cheese Shop
- 4 eggs
- 1 c. milk
- 1 c. whipping cream
- 1 T. flour
- ½ c. red onion chopped
- ½ c. chopped marinated artichokes
- 2 T. fresh rosemary chopped to garnish on the top
- 4 T. butter
- 1 10 inch baked pie shell

Preheat oven to 325°. Sauté onion in the butter until lightly brown. Spread onion mixture on the bottom of the pie shell. Add ham, then cheese to onion layer. Mix eggs, milk, cream and flour together in a large mixing bowl. Carefully pour mixture over cheese ham and onion layers.

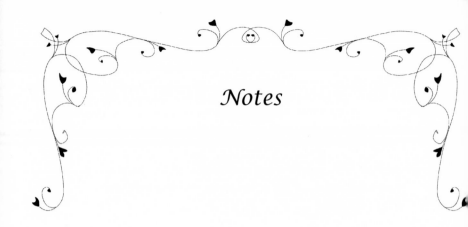

Notes

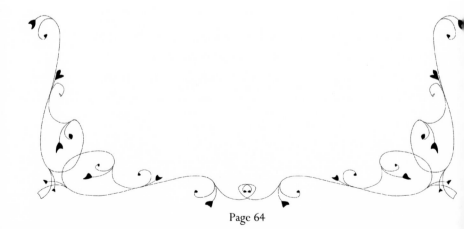

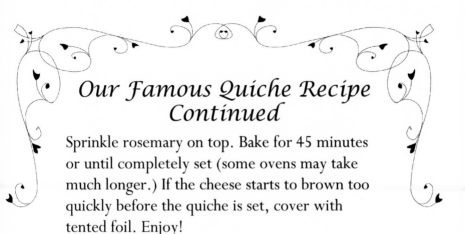

Our Famous Quiche Recipe
Continued

Sprinkle rosemary on top. Bake for 45 minutes or until completely set (some ovens may take much longer.) If the cheese starts to brown too quickly before the quiche is set, cover with tented foil. Enjoy!

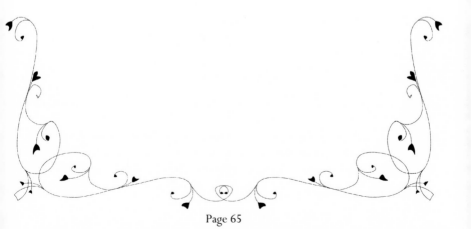

Notes

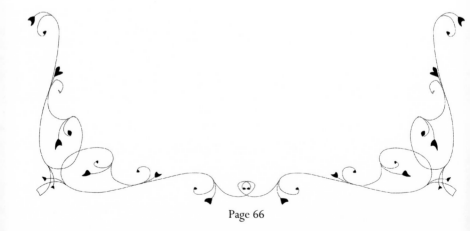

Soups

Tomato Basil Bisque

- ½ c. onion, finely chopped
- ¼ c. flour
- 4 c. tomatoes, finely chopped/pureed
- 1 t. dill seed
- 1 t. dill weed
- 1 t. oregano
- 3 c. chicken stock
- ¼ c. honey
- 1 c. cream
- ¼ c. chopped parsley
- ¼ c. chopped basil
- 4 T. butter

Sauté onions in butter.

Add flour, tomatoes, and spices. Add chicken stock and bring to a boil. Simmer for 15 minutes. Add honey, cream, parsley, and basil. Heat thoroughly. Add salt and pepper to taste.

Enjoy!

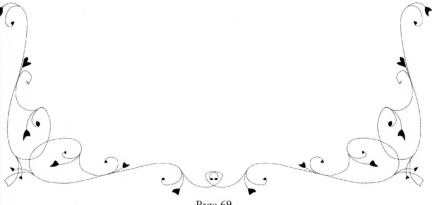

Notes

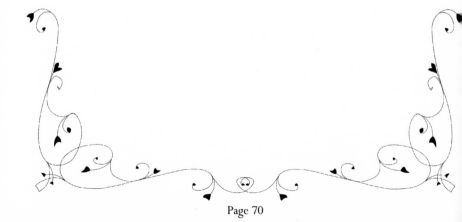

Roasted Carrot Soup

- 4 t. butter, melted
- ½ t. black pepper
- 2 pounds carrots cut into 2 inch pieces
- 1½ c. water
- 2 t. chopped oregano or ½ t. dried oregano
- 1 t. butter
- ½ t. cumin
- 1½ T. honey
- 1 T. fresh lime juice
- 2 (14½ oz.) can vegetable/chicken broth

Preheat oven to 400°. Combine 4 t. melted butter, pepper and carrots in a shallow roasting pan coated with cooking spray; toss to coat. Bake at 400° for 35 minutes or until tender, stirring every 10 minutes.

Place carrot mixture, water and oregano in a food processor, process until smooth.

Melt 1 t. butter in a large saucepan over medium heat. Add the cumin, cook 30 seconds or until fragrant, stirring constantly. Add pureed carrot mixture, honey, lime juice, and broth. Bring to a simmer over medium heat.

Makes 7 servings.

Notes

Salads

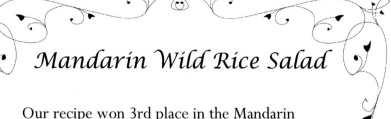

Mandarin Wild Rice Salad

Our recipe won 3rd place in the Mandarin Festival held in Auburn of November 2003.

- 1 c. wild rice
- 1 c. mandarin oranges
- ¼ c. green onions
- ½ c. dried cranberries
- ¼ c. toasted pecans
- ¼ c. freshly chopped mint
- ½ c. orange juice
- ¼ c. vegetable oil
- 1 t. salt
- dash of pepper

Cook wild rice according to package directions.

Add mandarins, onions, cranberries, pecans and mint. Combine orange juice, oil, salt and pepper in a small bowl. Pour over wild rice mixture. Let set at least 2 hours at room temperature before serving.

Enjoy!

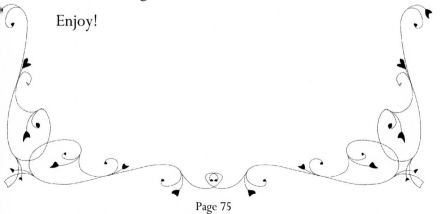

Notes

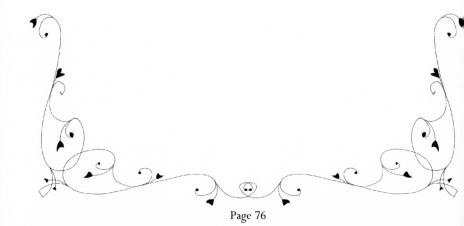

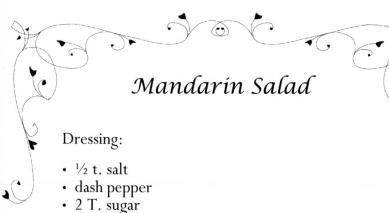

Mandarin Salad

Dressing:

- ½ t. salt
- dash pepper
- 2 T. sugar
- 2 T. vinegar
- ¼ c. oil
- dash red pepper sauce
- 1 T. parsley

Salad:

- ¼ c. sliced almonds
- 1½ T. sugar
- ¼ head of lettuce
- ¼ head romaine
- 1 c. chopped celery
- 2 green onions thinly sliced
- 1 can of mandarin oranges drained

Mix together dressing ingredients; refrigerate. Cook almonds and sugar over low heat. Stir until sugar is melted and almonds are coated. Cool; break apart. Store at room temperature.

Tear romaine and lettuce into bite size pieces (4 cups.) Place greens in plastic bag. Add celery

Notes

Mandarin Salad Continued

and onion. Seal bag and refrigerate. Five minutes before serving pour dressing into bag; add 1 can mandarin oranges, drained. Fasten bag and shake; add almonds.

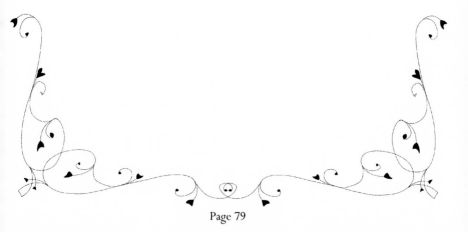

Notes

Strawberry Mango Spinach Salad

- ⅔ c. sugar
- 1 t. dry mustard
- ½ t. salt
- ⅓ c. honey
- 3 T. lemon juice
- 3 T. vinegar
- 2 t. grated onion
- 1 c. salad oil
- 1 T. poppy seeds
- Spinach
- ½ c. sliced strawberries
- ½ c. chopped mangoes

In blender mix first 3 ingredients. Add honey, lemon juice, vinegar and onion. Blend 1 minute until opaque in color. Pour oil in slowly. Add poppy seed.

In a large bowl, mix spinach, strawberries and mangoes. Add dressing and toss.

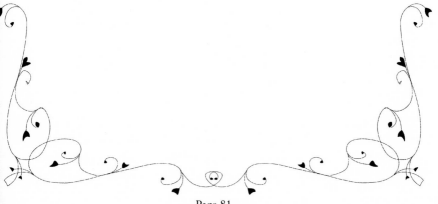

Notes

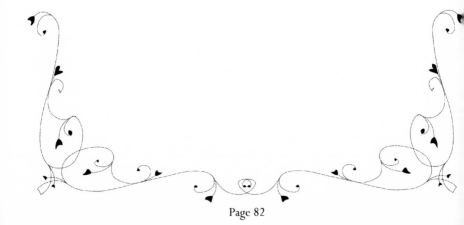

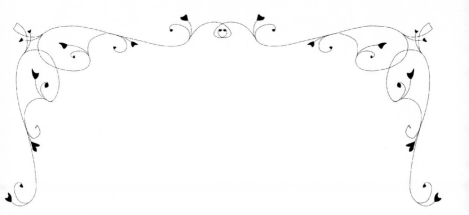

Tea Sandwiches

Introduction to Tea Sandwiches

Tea sandwiches can be made with just about any filling. Cutting the bread into interesting shapes using a cookie cutter really makes them unique. Tea sandwiches can be prepared in advance. Just make sure to store them in an airtight container lined with waxed paper and separate layers with lightly dampened paper towels.

Chicken sandwiches are one of our most popular items on our tea tray. There are endless combinations using cooked chicken. Connie and I try to come up with a new variation just about every week. Here are a few recipes to help you get started. Have fun creating your own.

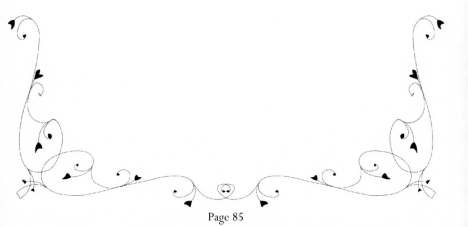

Apple Walnut Chicken Sandwiches

- 2 c. cooked chicken
- 1 apple sliced and chopped
- 1 T. lemon juice
- ¼ c. walnuts
- 3 green onions sliced thinly
- Mayonnaise
- Butter
- Bread
- Parsley

Mix together first five ingredients. Add just enough mayonnaise to bind mixture together. Spread butter on bread. Add filling and top with second slice. Cut into desired shapes-squares, triangles, etc. Butter sides and dip into dried parsley for decoration.

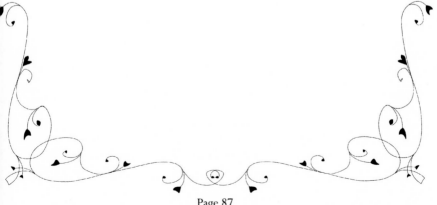

Notes

Caesar Chicken Sandwiches

- 2 c. cooked chicken
- 1 garlic clove minced
- 3 T. toasted almonds
- 3 T. parmesan cheese, grated
- Mayonnaise
- Parsley
- Butter
- Bread

Mix together first four ingredients. Add just enough mayonnaise to bind mixture together. Spread butter on bread. Add filling and top with second slice. Cut into desired shapes-squares, triangles, etc. Butter sides and dip into parsley and extra parmesan cheese.

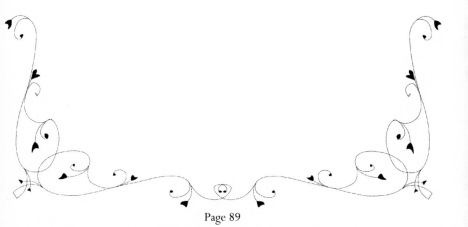

Notes

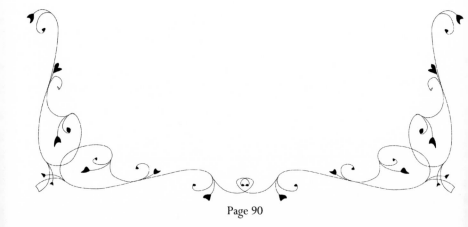

Cranberry Chicken Salad Sandwiches

- 2 c. cooked chicken
- ½ c. cranberries, sliced or dried
- ¼ c. cup pecans
- 3 green onions, sliced
- Mayonnaise
- White or wheat bread slices
- Butter
- Parsley for decoration

In a large bowl, combine first 4 ingredients. Add just enough mayonnaise to moisten. Cover and chill to blend flavors.

Butter 2 slices of bread. Spread enough chicken salad mixture on one of the buttered slices to make a thick sandwich. Cover with remaining top slice. Repeat with remaining slices of bread.

For best tea sandwich results, chill for at least 30 minutes before cutting. Trim off bread crusts and cut into triangles or squares. Keep covered with a moist paper towel or in an airtight container until ready to serve.

Notes

Macadamia Chicken Sandwiches

- 4 c. cooked, cubed chicken
- 20 oz. can pineapple chunks, drained
- 1 c. Macadamia nuts, halved or cut in quarters
- ½ c. thinly sliced celery
- ¼ t. ginger
- 1 c. mayonnaise

In a large bowl, combine first 4 ingredients.
Combine ginger and mayonnaise, mixing well.
Add just enough mayonnaise to moisten.

Cover and chill to blend flavors.

Notes

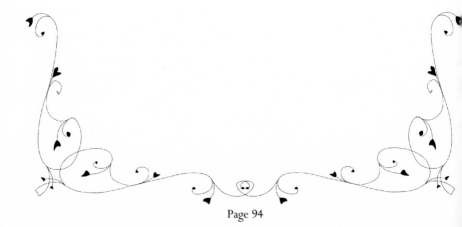

Sesame Chicken Sandwiches

- 2 c. cooked chicken
- 2 T. sesame seed oil
- 3 T. green onions, sliced thinly
- ¼ c. chopped cilantro
- Mayonnaise
- Sesame seeds
- Butter
- Bread

Mix together first four ingredients. Add just enough mayonnaise to bind mixture together. Spread butter on bread. Add filling and top with second slice. Cut into desired shapes-squares, triangles, etc. Butter sides and dip into sesame seeds for decoration.

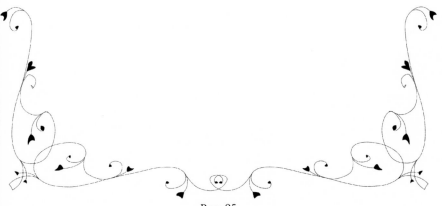

Notes

Tarragon Chicken Sandwiches

- 2 c. cooked chicken
- 1 T. tarragon
- 1 T. lemon juice
- 3 T. toasted almonds
- Mayonnaise
- Parsley
- Butter
- Bread

Mix together first four ingredients. Add just enough mayonnaise to bind mixture together. Spread butter on bread. Add filling and top with second slice. Cut into desired shapes – squares, triangles, etc. Butter sides and dip into dried parsley for decoration.

Hint: The sandwiches cut better if they are chilled an hour before cutting.

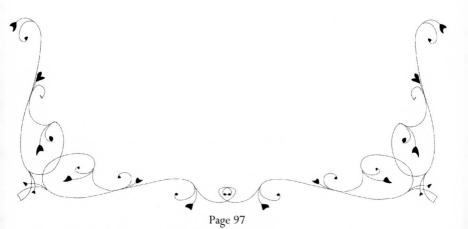

Notes

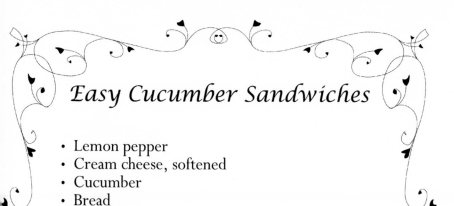

Easy Cucumber Sandwiches

- Lemon pepper
- Cream cheese, softened
- Cucumber
- Bread

Spread cream cheese on bread slices. Place 4-5 cucumber slices over cream cheese. Sprinkle lemon pepper on top. Top with remaining bread slice. Cut into desired shapes.

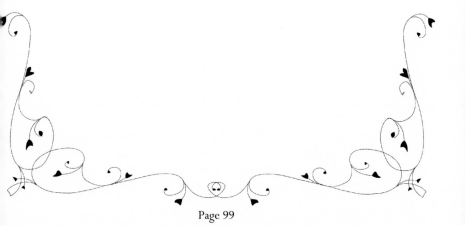

Notes

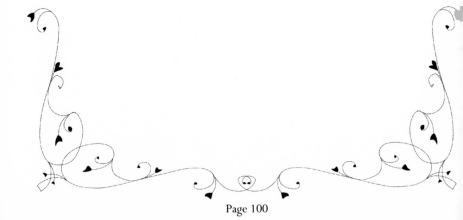

Lisa's Open-Faced Cucumber Sandwiches

- 3 oz. cream cheese
- ½ small onion
- 1 t. lemon juice
- Cucumber
- ¼ c. sour cream
- ¼ c. mayonnaise
- Lawrey's Seasoning salt
- Bread

Grate ½ small onion. Mix softened cream cheese, onion, and lemon juice. Butter bread and spread with cream cheese mix. Run a fork down the sides of a cucumber. Slice. Pack slices on ice. Mix equal parts of sour cream and mayonnaise. Put cucumber on bread, add a spoon of sour cream and mayonnaise mix. Sprinkle with Lawrey's Seasoning Salt. Cutting the bread first with a tea pot cookie cutter really makes these sandwiches stand out on a tea tray.

Notes

Corned Beef Sandwiches

- 1 3 oz. package cream cheese, softened
- ¼ c. onion, finely chopped
- ¼ c. water chesnuts, finely chopped
- 1 T. mustard
- 2 t. prepared horseradish
- ⅛ t. salt
- Dash pepper
- 6 oz. shaved corned beef, chopped
- 8 slices of pumpernickel bread or rye bread
- Butter, softened

Combine cheese, onion, water chestnuts, mustard, horseradish, salt and pepper. Stir in corned beef. Spread 4 slices of bread with butter. Spread half with corned beef mixture and top with remaining halves. Freeze if desired. Makes 4 large sandwiches (regular size) or 24 tea sandwiches.

To freeze: Place each sandwich in a Ziplock bag. Sandwiches may be kept frozen for 2 weeks. Thaw before serving.

Notes

Egg Salad with Dill

- 8 hard cooked eggs
- ½ c. finely chopped red onion
- ⅓ c. chopped fresh dill
- ½ c. mayonnaise
- ¼ c. sour cream
- ¼ c. Dijon-style mustard
- Salt and freshly ground black pepper to taste

Peel the eggs and quarter them. Place in a mixing bowl with the onion and the dill. In another bowl whisk together the mayonnaise, sour cream and mustard and pour over the eggs, onion and dill. Toss gently, season to taste with salt and pepper. Cover and refrigerate.

Salad is best eaten immediately.

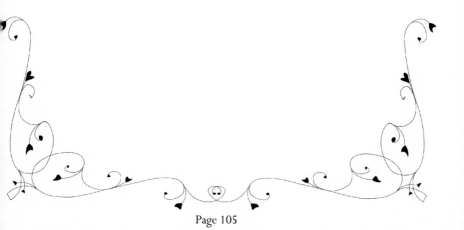

Notes

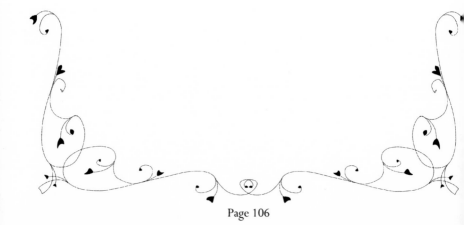

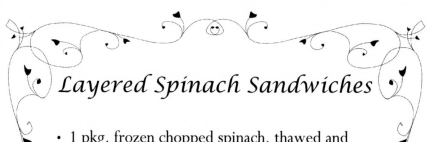

Layered Spinach Sandwiches

- 1 pkg. frozen chopped spinach, thawed and squeezed dry
- 1 pkg. dry vegetable soup mix
- 1 small carton sour cream
- 1 small can water chestnuts, chopped
- 1 small jar pimento
- 8 oz. sharp cheddar cheese, grated
- 1 c. mayonnaise
- 3 oz. cream cheese, softened
- Pepper to taste
- White and wheat or rye bread slices

Make spinach mixture by combining dry soup mix with sour cream and mayonnaise. Add thawed spinach that has the excess water removed. Add chopped water chestnuts . Drain pimento and add remaining ingredients.

To assemble sandwiches, spread a rye slice of bread with the spinach mixture. Top with a wheat or rye slice, then spread with another layer of the spinach mixture. Top again with another slice of rye. These are very pretty 3 layer ribbon sandwiches.

Notes

Desserts

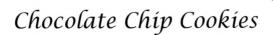

Chocolate Chip Cookies

- 1 c. butter
- ½ c. shortening
- 2 c. dark brown sugar firmly packed
- 2 eggs
- 1 T. vanilla
- 2 c. flour
- 1 t. baking soda
- ½ t. salt
- 2 c. oatmeal
- 2 c. crisp rice cereal
- 1 c. shredded coconut
- 1 c. chopped walnuts
- 2 c. semi-sweet chocolate chips

Preheat oven to 350°. Combine butter, shortening, brown sugar, eggs and vanilla in large bowl. Beat at medium speed of electric mixer until well blended.

Combine flour, baking soda and salt. Add gradually to creamed mixture at low speed. Stir in oats, rice cereal, coconut, nuts and chocolate chips with spoon. Drop by heaping teaspoonfuls 2 inches apart onto ungreased baking sheet.

Notes

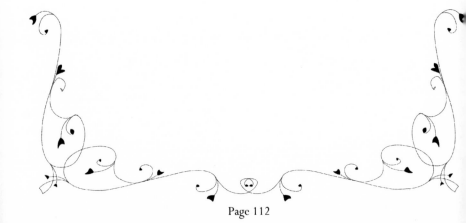

Chocolate Chip Cookies
Continued

Bake at 350° for 10-12 minutes or until light brown and just set in center. Cool 1 minute on baking sheet before removing to cooling rack.

Makes about 7 ½ dozen cookies.

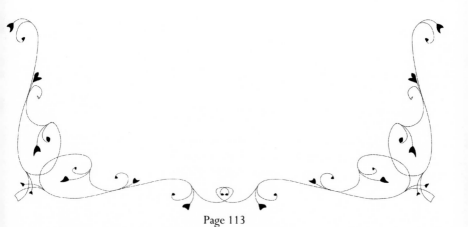

Notes

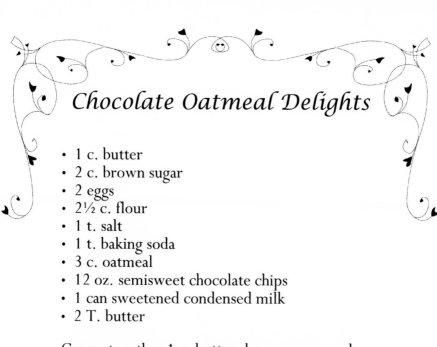

Chocolate Oatmeal Delights

- 1 c. butter
- 2 c. brown sugar
- 2 eggs
- 2½ c. flour
- 1 t. salt
- 1 t. baking soda
- 3 c. oatmeal
- 12 oz. semisweet chocolate chips
- 1 can sweetened condensed milk
- 2 T. butter

Cream together 1 c. butter, brown sugar and eggs. Sift together flour, salt and baking soda. Add to creamed mixture. Stir in oatmeal. Press ¾ of mixture into a 9" x 13" pan. (Reserve the remaining ¼ mixture.) Melt together chocolate chips, sweetened condensed milk and 2 T. butter. Pour over oatmeal mixture. Crumble/chunk the reserved oatmeal mixture on the top of the chocolate mixture. Bake at 350° for 20 minutes. Do not over bake. Let set for a few hours before cutting.

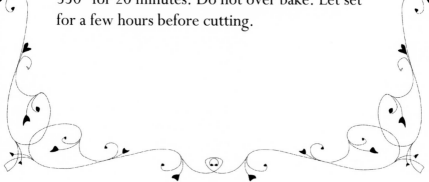

Notes

Connie's Famous Fudge

- 2 c. semisweet chocolate chips
- 1 c. white chocolate chips
- 1 can sweetened condensed milk
- ¼ c. butter
- 1 c. walnuts, chopped

Place all ingredients except nuts in large bowl. Microwave at MEDIUM (50%) until chocolate chips are melted, 3 to 5 minutes, stirring once or twice during cooking. Stir in nuts. Pour into a well-greased square baking dish, 8" x 8". Refrigerate until set.

Notes

Coconut Macaroons

- 1 15 oz. package coconut
- 1 can sweetened condensed milk
- 1 t. vanilla
- 1 c. semisweet chocolate chips, melted

Mix coconut, vanilla and sweetened condensed milk in a large bowl. Drop by spoonfuls onto a cookie sheet lined with parchment paper. Bake at 350° for 10 minutes or until set.

When cool, drizzle melted chocolate chips over top for decoration.

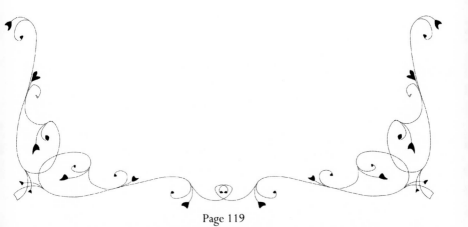

Notes

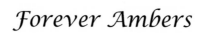

Forever Ambers

My grandmother used to make this candy every Christmas.

- 1 large package of orange sliced candy
- 1 16 oz. package of coconut
- 2 cans sweetened condensed milk
- 1 c. chopped nuts
- 1 t. orange flavoring
- 1 t. vanilla
- 1 16 oz. package of powdered sugar

Cut orange slices in small pieces. Mix candy, coconut, milk, nuts, orange flavoring and vanilla and spread into a greased 9" x 13" pan. Bake at 275° for 15 minutes. Stir and bake an additional 15 minutes. Remove from oven and sift the entire 16 oz. package of powdered sugar over mixture. Stir and drop by tablespoons onto waxed paper. Allow candy to dry and set.

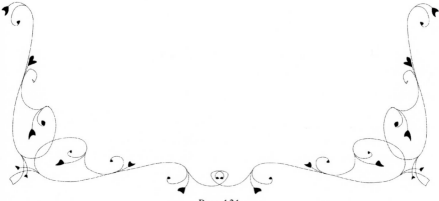

Notes

Granny's Cinnamon Apples

- 1 c. sugar
- 1 c. water
- 1 qt. peeled apples
- 1 lemon sliced
- 2 t. cinnamon

Combine sugar and water and bring to a boil.
Add apples, cover and cook slowly until syrup
boils; continue cooking gently pressing the
apples down occasionally with a spoon until they
are tender and transparent looking (about 30
minutes.) Slice lemon very thin and add to hot
syrup along with the spices. Serve in their own
syrup cold or hot.

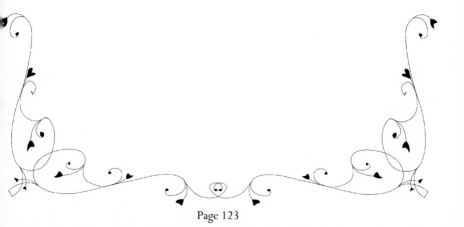

Notes

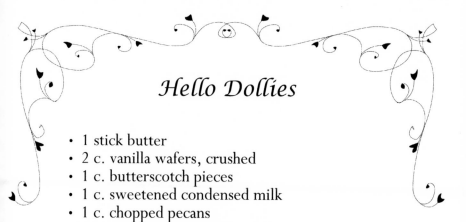

Hello Dollies

- 1 stick butter
- 2 c. vanilla wafers, crushed
- 1 c. butterscotch pieces
- 1 c. sweetened condensed milk
- 1 c. chopped pecans
- 1 c. semisweet chocolate chips
- 1 c. coconut

Melt butter in a 9" x 13" pan. Add vanilla wafers. Press in bottom of pan and add coconut, chips, and pecans. Pour sweetened condensed milk over the top. Bake at 350° for 25 minutes. Cool and cut into 1" squares.

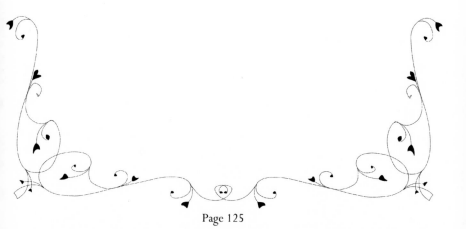

Notes

Lemon/Lime Raspberry Bars

- 1 c. butter softened
- ½ c. powdered sugar
- 2 c. flour
- 6 eggs
- 2¼ c. granulated sugar
- ¾ c. lemon juice or lime juice
- ½ c. flour
- 1½ t. baking powder
- ½ c. raspberry jam
- ½ c. white chocolate chips

Preheat oven to 350°. Beat butter in a large mixing bowl until fluffy. Beat in powdered sugar. Gradually add 2 c. of flour. Press dough into the bottom of a greased 9" x 13" inch pan. Bake 15-18 minutes until light brown.

Combine eggs, granulated sugar, lemon juice, ½ c. flour and baking powder in large bowl. Beat well. Pour over hot crust and bake 25 minutes or until set and top is golden. Remove from oven.

Heat jam in microwave or on stove until melted. Spread carefully over lemon bars. Cool

Notes

Lemon/Lime Raspberry Bars
Continued

completely. Melt white chips in microwave or on stove, drizzle over cooled bars. Store in refrigerator. Makes about 30 bars.

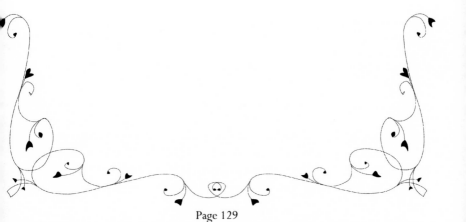

Notes

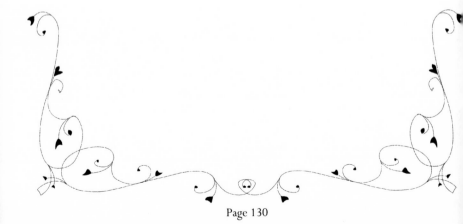

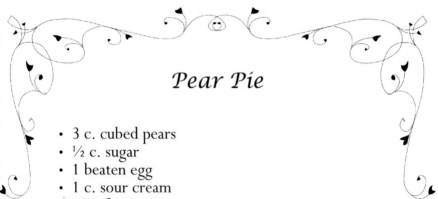

Pear Pie

- 3 c. cubed pears
- ½ c. sugar
- 1 beaten egg
- 1 c. sour cream
- 1 T. flour
- 1 t. vanilla
- ½ t. salt
- 1 unbaked pie shell

Crumb mix topping

- ⅔ c. flour
- ⅓ c. brown sugar
- ¼ c. butter

Combine sugar, egg, flour, vanilla and salt. Mix. Fold in sour cream and pears. Pour into shell. Bake at 350° for 15 minutes. Remove. Sprinkle crumb mix on top, return to oven and bake 30 minutes more or until brown.

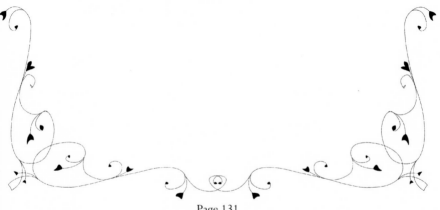

Notes

Rum Cake

Cake

- 1 Duncan Hines Moist Deluxe Butter Recipe
- 4 eggs
- ½ c. water
- ½ c. oil
- ½ c. rum

Glaze

- ¼ c. rum
- ¼ c. butter
- Dash of water
- 1 c. sugar

Preheat oven to 350°.

Prepare cake according to cake mix directions using the ingredients above. Bake at 350° in a bundt pan for 45-50 minutes or until done.

Glaze:

Combine ¼ c. rum, ¼ c. butter, dash of water and sugar in a small saucepan. Bring to a boil. Pour ½ mixture over cake while still hot. Let sit for 10 minutes. Invert cake on a serving plate. Brush on remaining glaze and let cool.

Notes

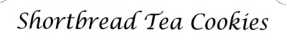

Shortbread Tea Cookies

- 1 c. butter
- ½ c. sugar
- 2¾ c. flour (add ½ cup at a time)
- ¼ c. dry, loose leaf tea-crushed (Rooibus – which is a tisane works very well, you could use just about any – Earl Grey is another favorite)
- ¼ t. salt

Preheat over to 350°.

Cream butter and sugar. Add in tea and salt. Gradually add flour a little at a time just until dough is no longer sticky. You may not need all the flour. Divide dough into 3 sections. Roll out on wax paper into a snake-like roll. Prick with fork and cut about into 1 inch pieces.

Bake at 350° about 10-12 minutes. Do not let brown.

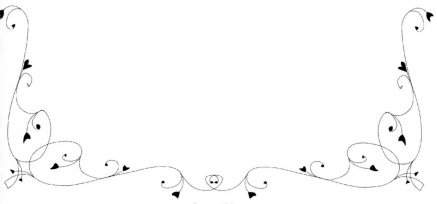

Notes

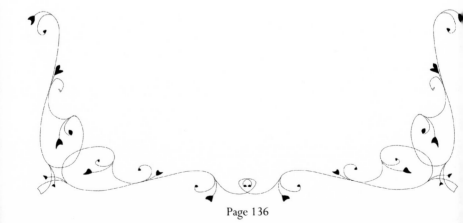

Index

Index Continued

About the Author

Amy Lawrence began her tea room in August of 2003. Previously she had been a special education teacher for 11 years teaching learning disabled and autistic students. She took a two year break to be home with her two sons. In August of 2002 while having tea with my mother, she said, "This is what I want to do now! I want my own tea room. I love to cook and have always enjoyed catering for special parties." In November of 2002, she attended a tea conference and also became a certified tea consultant. It all began from there. With the help of dedicated family and friends, she finally opened her tea room on August 27, 2003. In July 2006, Tea Experience Digest named An Afternoon to Remember Tea Parlor and Gifts the Reader's Choice Award for Best Small City Tea Room in the U.S. At the present time, Amy has self-published 4 cookbooks and is currently working on a new book on afternoon teas.

Breinigsville, PA USA
16 March 2011
257787BV00001B/289/A